echolalia echolalia

Jane Shi

echolalia echolalia

jane shi

BRICK BOOKS

Library and Archives Canada Cataloguing in Publication

Title: Echolalia echolalia / Jane Shi.
Names: Shi, Jane, author.
Identifiers: Canadiana (print) 20240402871 | Canadiana (ebook) 20240402928 | ISBN 9781771316378
(softcover) | ISBN 9781771316385 (EPUB) | ISBN 9781771316392 (PDF)
Subjects: LCGFT: Poetry.
Classification: LCC PS8637.H4898 E34 2024 | DDC C811/.6—dc23

We gratefully acknowledge the Canada Council for the Arts, the Government of Canada through the Canada Book Fund, and the Ontario Arts Council and the Government of Ontario for their support of our publishing program.

Edited by Phoebe Wang.

Cover image by Jia Sung (*snake eater*, 2021).
Author photo by Divya Kaur.

The book is set in Baskerville and Futura.
Design by Emma Allain.

Brick Books
487 King St. W.
Kingston, ON
K7L 2X7
www.brickbooks.ca

Though much of the work of Brick Books takes place on the ancestral lands of the Anishinaabeg, Haudenosaunee, Huron-Wendat, and Mississaugas of the Credit peoples, our editors, authors, and readers from many backgrounds are situated from coast to coast to coast in Canada on the traditional and unceded territories of over six hundred nations who have cared for Turtle Island from time immemorial. While living and working on these lands, we are committed to hearing and returning the rightful imaginative space to the poetries, songs, and stories that have been untold, under-told, wrongly told, and suppressed through colonization.

for the mouths sewed shut
    mumbling water   what water

contents

so much time   waiting

is not a passive

act it will take

a pleating

skin shell

to swallow hole

g h o s t

culinary 32.8%

superstitious **36.4%**

deeply scientific 9.6%

religious 21.2%

in relation to your waiting room are you

Unreliable ~~Nar~~Reader

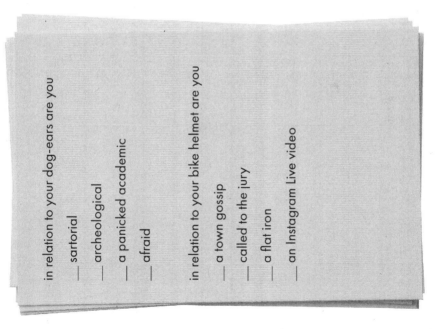

in relation to your dog-ears are you

___ sartorial

___ archeological

___ a panicked academic

___ afraid

in relation to your bike helmet are you

___ a town gossip

___ called to the jury

___ a flat iron

___ an Instagram Live video

Reading Practice

This page pecks worms from my pocket eyes. She
              knows I haven't done the readings. She gnaws

at the underbelly: bubble bat zaps
              electrolocation darts with theory

daggers, grammar taunts. My back balances
              the expectations of a white Lady

of the Cloud Firmament, silly putties
              pipe-cleaner people into a cardboard

corporate strip mall roundabout. Wonder
              -land somewhere breathable. Twelve-year-old me

chants, *Bike away forever.* Reading these
              measurements at the same time as reading

my palms is a reading practice. Little
              post-its of reject grammatology.

              I eat paint chips, flush out stitches. As if
to say, *Swish!* None of it was done to me.

              I bathe in the noise album of bookstore
cash machines, use non-profit loofas to

              wipe away the grime. Ballpoint pen shampoo
my copy of *Norton Anthology*

              of English Shiterature. I take notes

so Auncle Time won't have to use their hands.

             I store clocks in the freezer until I'm
ready to defrost my face in the sink.

             Wait for them to chide me for not doing
it right. I haven't done the readings

             but I taped a book inside the creases
around my eyes. Here: if you squeeze in fast

enough you might catch me breathing. Sputters
             of dirt, growth, hills among a thousand years

of jarred bayberry scholarship. Read me.

Industry of Language

listen there are tricks   to trade
to learning (主ing)   character
worksheets to photocopy   true friend
ditties umbilical   verses
to rubber duck   a mirror
to polish then cut   corner
a solemn doorstopper   collapses
this experiment's   wily
trick: the door was closed   & cryptic
when 爸 happened   like that
to mistake it for you   *snap!*

say cheese / say charm

anaesthetize the subject
floss out the sibilant
adjust the digraph
debride her wisdom
avulse the voiced
from voiceless
geometry a friction
pulls back her hair
until she smiles
perfect
stenciled parenthetical

crooked
corn dirt
pincers pinched perilous
pock-door sun-worn
undulating parts
unprecious stone
speech glint starry red
strokes flying   flags
fracture   fogs of

not surrendering

stomatologist tests
mispronounces potatoes
denounces a riff-raff
run-on gargle system
do not disappoint
daughterhood awful
jargle non-fiction
I can't help it I live here
inside the cavities

for the camera   of ugly

playing cards
warm dust
printed mosquitos
torpedo pearl unfurl
proton a clothesline
someone else a crier
me-slipped sorry mess
yes yes   absolutely
magnet rubble for

not surrendering

fox eye drops

　　　dare you　　　wolf eyes　　　that flay　　like mine
when they　　twin keyholes　　common law
　　dewdrops　　　　outlet in a yellowing　　　　　　wall

burnt down　　a crayon city　　weather
　　so antarctica　　　have seen　　so much?

huli jing glances　　　　bridged with large brown
　　　brushes & broomstick bristle　　bangs　a rock
　gun closed of lost sticks　　& rubber bands

　　　i got this dollop of sadness
from him

My grandfather collected shit

No, my grandmother's the one who collects
things. But it was my grandfather who once used
a bucket to gather & dump human

leftovers from the clogged squat
toilets of the country's leaping bowels. Now, eyes
moon-lifted, he fits air conditioners across ceilings

of modernity, banks on more & more sky
scrapers like silver quills mined from porcupine
graves, couldn't once apologize for leaving   ·

a mother, two children, an army
of slippers to collect debts of broken
furniture, fishbone tails of rare

ditch bruises. Descended from hap
hazard neglect, it's no wonder I'd leave Chang'e
on read, too. On WeChat, goddess's toilet

paper gown drifts across a purple Pacific, clean
mist of sacrifice translates automatically: *Look! The garbage
patch of shit your grandfather collected. I helped.*

how do u say help me in yr language
how much ginseng do u take each morning
how do u say fed up in yr language
what's yr favourite tea
how do u say no more in yr language
did u like these dumplings i made u
what colour is precious in yr language
how much baijiu do i pour u
can u hear the cicadas in yr language
do u like this painting i made
what storms do i part in yr language
what do u think of corn oh oh oh
what of u am i holding in yr language
how do u fold yr dumplings tho
what do i let go of in yr language
n what about this pomegranate
what will it take in yr language
how do u do yr hair
what would disappoint yr language
how do u like yr spices
how do u stay in yr language
i really like donut peaches
do i keep searching in yr language
do u like them too
how would u pronounce my name

how to let someone in

I am a mildew flower / I am a
                    smoking porch / I am a mushroom
          failing to forget / I am a *Kingdom*
     Hearts OST you play in the background / I am a battery
   inside a calculator waiting to run out / I am a sound
-proof wall / I am a three-week stand with nighttime / I am
oranges & bamboo plants & succulents / I am a sink falling
     apart / I am a corner
                    where you shiver so hotly / I am a jam jar
on the sex-toy shelf / I am a drill against delicate
knuckles / I am finger tapping blades of grass / I am egg
     -tart flakes / I am a whimper / I am   a sharp edge

                    I am not a weekly check
          -in / I am not enough light   for the monstera
                    plant / I am not half-baked
     apologies / I am not a teddy bear / I am not vitamins
          for going vegan / I am not a contract
                    for ceiling popcorn / I am not a contest
     anyone can win / I am not a rug / I am not a stove
          struggling for breath / I am not the right condition
     to choose / I am not a bridge
                    of magnolias

I am magnolias / I am totally one-sided / I am desperate
approximations of uvula /   I am a toilet
plunger / I am flush / I am deteriorating
paint / I am throat-full of dust / I am plastic wrap
over a TV dinner / I am unforgiving
drafts / I am so impossible the city would collapse / I am pencil
splinters staying in skin / I am a bouquet
of tissues / I am blackberry gumdrop /
I am your love me anyway

/ I am your come on in! /
I am your stay a little longer it's still early /
I am your dewdrop drown / I am how
/ I am how

Definition Hostile

family

is not father

                                                  not mother

not a conjunction   or

                a means   an end

not

               I   L   Y

but a calculus of nation & resignation

complex   PTSD

is an apartment on Azure lu & yanping Road

hidden haunted

dollhouse

               festers in tenderloin

               ho stil e arch   i tec   ture

is the absurdity of banking
all yr slot machine plastic coins on

mildew

is a rotation of bees
in a heap of concrete

is glued-together obligations

pity is petty
is
piety is
as easy as pie

piety

is a slather of choices
Colonial St.

Regent House

men's mattresses
choosing for you

choice

is easy as pie
if it means dipping like the biggest dipper

the biggest dipper
is
the obsolescence
of piracy   &   privacy

privacy is a poem
that subtweets
yr upbringing

bringing is giving
too much away

away is away
from the chat
away from her
childhood
a way's a way

too much is an excuse
for what
we do among
ourselves

what is
time
for something different

'different' is so annoying lol

time is
a heptapod's
text messages thru space

(is it problematic for
the beginning of the universe
to flirt with the end of the universe
if they are roommates)

the end
is
every time you sigh

signs are finger
tapping the chords
for the   years
it took to walk yr way across
one feeling

is
feeling

race is

not a face
not a chase
not a lace
not a taste
not a maze
not a lake
not a way
not a vase
not a day
not a quay

a key
is
a stim toy
you hide in yr crotch
so you won't have to go back

back
is
a canvas for tattoos
not hands
not levers

a lever
is
leaving you to face it

a face can't be saved

before you were born

with gratitude to Diana Khoi Nguyen

what would y
ou say to me if yo
u knew the truth if yo
er ou would open the way
e ne ce ssa ry to keep you th os
tell them what you could
id you want to protect me
from you want to tell me
ger remain a world that too d on
y exist this year made ever
of things you would not w
se me do you would do
seeme look at yoo
ung place me now
aabbl

the face o
f history
stairs this sacrets
me still black
you
u
aff
e

who holds
up this portra
it & with
pqens
e
ayes
s
d

Fig. 1: ~~they offered you~~

27

Fig. 2: cartridge of lies

what would y
ou say to me if yo
u knew me then if y
ou could open the wat
er of your eyes & choos
e me as i am if you could
tell me why what stories d
id you want to protect me
from a world that no lon
ger exists time made ever
ything disappear you w
orried you would lo
se me i look at yo
ur face now
a bl

the face o
f history secrets
stairs blankly mo
ment to moment &
you kept looking yo
u refused to look b
affling ascent of th
e camera flash ca
rtridge of ligh

who holds
up this portra
it & with what s
poons do we lift th
e cranes toothpick gr
aves poking from mos
s mosquito tent scaffol
dings he wasn't there f
or her when she fell s
he wanted to protect
me from the absenc
e of the fishing vi
llage the cold
air of

griefcase

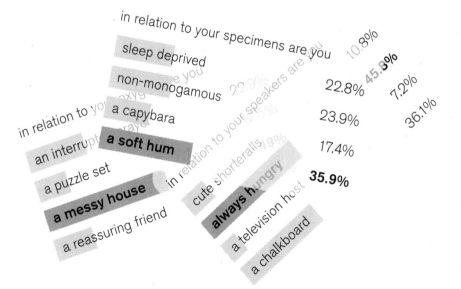

in relation to your specimens are you

sleep deprived

non-monogamous

a capybara

an interrupt... **a soft hum**

a puzzle set

a messy house

a reassuring friend

in relation to your speakers are you

cute shorteralls **always hungry**

a television host

a chalkboard

10.8%   **45.8%**   7.2%

22.8%   36.1%

22.9%

23.9%

17.4%

35.9%

back in a nanosec
after Tank and the Bangas' "Rollercoasters"

Hi Bonnie! It's been a couple
    of months (almost two summers if

        you're counting, right?) & I just wanted
            to ask if we're still for-a-long-time

                pals. What do you think a long time means,
                  anyway? Last night as I was lying

      in bed my face grew into a basket
    of wind that remembered the back

& forth of that pirate ride at Playland.
    I like the predictability of it

        & was just wondering how
           you felt about being a particular

              kind of pirate ship predictable
           with me. I don't mind

              the brief uncertainty of suspension.
                I don't mind the out-of-body

              sensation of the drop. I don't
           mind doing it again & again & again,

              wondering if the earth is just a pendulum
        that has broken from its fulcrum.

Bonnie, Bonnie—remember when we
        would huddle together in the dark, so glad

to finally unfurl into each other's hunger?
        Drank our enemies' apples,

                irises & mouse traps, how they
                        almost dispersed our every atom until we

                                forgot what it meant to watch bad anime
                                        on our shared Crunchyroll account or sit

                                        with our dewdrop lids? I want
                                to put out my fear of heights & ride

                that improbable oversized boat on the waves
        of cotton candy vomit & giant teddy Pikachus

with you. But if you don't want to,
        that's okay. I don't mind. Maybe

the reason you don't need me anymore is we needed
        to trick ourselves. It's like that with everything

        isn't it? How scary it's been to ride
                that pirate ship alone. Oh, it's 4:21am already.

                I guess you only live a few kilometers away
                        so it's 4:21am for you as well. I'm

                just a few nanoseconds in the future.
                        In the future, I still miss you

                though at a slightly different angle. I want to
                        look beside me & know that you're

close when we fall. I wish we could go
look at the booths of the carnival

    & buy cute bookmarks like we did that
one summer—last time I bought a new

        keychain though. See? To keep
      us safe on the pirate ship. We can hold it

            tight & know in our bellies the fall
               & swing are temporary. We'll go up.

                  We'll come down. Riding that boat
                    for a long time, won't we?

Pirated DVDs Are My Cousins
for Nurdoukht Khudonazarova Taghdumbashi

I want to download you, then store you
    in a hard drive so tough the Juan de Fuca

        Plate can't break it. I am in it, holding
            you, an empty bell in the middle,

            so prismatic clicks of kaleidoscope
                enter through the J-cut, burn it

                to find you, splice in a bicycle
                cart down the corridor, used Lego

                -piece pink apartments. Approach me
                with eagerness for the impossible

            purchase of new life. Sweet moons,
        I should have stolen more of you

        when I had the chance. To love
    in the girth of the mountains. Regret is

obsolescence with a purpose. Can't watch
you now. No, won't rewind you, either.

Deep Inside You're Just a Tool Fan

You never grew up. The timbres
   of MJK's reedy aged-wine hollers
   kept you from an early death. You're
      as cerebral as DC's large-muscled
         drum heartbeats. Which are also crop
            circles AJ carved in the atmosphere.
                 What the frick does bass do, you dunno

but JC must be the prickly pear
   texture of the galaxy's sonic weighted
   blanket. I wouldn't say Tool is Buddhist
      but they're also not not Buddhist, know
         what I mean? This won't be the last
            bit you bump into yourself in blank
               verse. I & you crowd surfing giddily,

you carrying I across the arena. You
   take the only thing that soothes
   your broken bodymind: Jambi at full
      volume, biking across the dike, watching
         the stars flicker & wink like cellphones
            at the show. Who cares what 46 & 2
               really means; it slaps & you slapped

yourself with sound until both ears
　　almost shatter because that's how
　　you conduct EMDR on I when I
　　　　really needed it. Body blasts the Tool
　　　　　　score. Thrum, thrum, boom. Tap, tap.
　　　　　　　　You change the lyrics to be as queer

as possible. Tag your dating profile
　　with #ToolFan4ToolFan. Refer
　　to yourself as he/him occasionally.
　　　　No one else gets it but that's not
　　　　　　the point. The point is that metal is
　　　　　　　　prayer & odd time signatures holding
　　　　　　　　　　you when no one else would, the swirls
　　　　　　　　　your lungs draw like particle handwriting:
　　　　　the only place you're sure of yourself,
　　　　being alone without being alone.

worship the exit light

*A found poem created
from my wordpress poetry journal
of my late teens (2008-2010)*

a tide-pool winter a hiss
of hot violets little fibres
along my bedspread brush of threaded grass
in the grubby broken cinema of memory scrub
my back filthily in the thick sublunary lust
stars would make canyons o me the vast valleys
airless marshes where travellers stumbled
as they sought false light the world
will shift into an upward crescent
a dusty friction the lifespan of our
teeth is only about thirty shoe buckle being my
granddadaddy i'm a peachpit in a crow's mouth
crowded angry skins are pulled off so i play
loud music to drown out their false concern
worship the exit light lips tied faster
how do you know you love someone
eating saltine crackers for breakfast every day
the solar system is unstable taps
temple i don't need my shoes shined
energetic fulcrum tips
didn't feel very journalistic today
wars never

i want to face consequences

After Kai Cheng Thom

                  17
                years
              old, and
            still throwing
          tantrums. the suburban
        problem so specifically
      misdiagnosed
    as the problem
  of picky eating. on a sunday 10
years later she'll check
into a resignation hostel. become
an audible ghost, beckon a make-believe
social worker to arrive at her pillowside like a tooth
fairy. the perfect answer she's prepared for tinker
bell: "i will find the right
words to anyone who will listen, anyone
  who will listen." not an excuse
    for frightening the neighbours. grey
      toyota more toy car than allwheeldrive. her raggedy
        doll parents run out   of words, muffled
          arguments like code
            that refused to compile. somewhere along river
              road she's become a stanza of javascript. "i want you
                to get me my inconsequential things." joints
                  squeak against gravel, still comforting. she'll
                    remember that quiznos sandwich years later.   pickles,
                        olives, mayonnaise. "i want you to go   out
                            and find me, find me   and bring
                                me home."

loves'eat

that fall she dreamt about
new baby teeth, mixing up
a tornado with eucalyptus
plant. a blur of words cast
on her forehead, brilliant in
the mirror where moonlight

forgot to shine. she spread
her quiet legs across a cliff
rested against soft breaths
breaking. where his 2-part
IKEA couch met like long
lost jade rings split in the

heat of war-drenched passion. that night, she plucked off
chestnuts fresh from his fridge. her mouth was filthy
from telling the truth. you see, she just needed to lie
down for a little while. dream-teeth crevice between
the aches. pasts. lives. startled inside the oven. tender
baby-fists warm to the touch. she bit sleepily into them.

bellytide

gallium cangue
        you were four
     doctor saw
   bones another eye
          drop meniscus sand
             -box for wanting
     more than what
    was given
              diminutive medea
   glugs bathwater devotion
            i won't kill
another baby i won't   promise   she will be a good good

mother i can't   help
       watch as she returns
     those harsh contractions beckoning you whiplash
of possession   a thousand jasons won't

   fill   scab
      scab   scarlet hand   let me void
this refund   spam
      shouxing's inbox   forcep me
    would this stipulation   curettage me medea
    my killer my mother who slipped
in the stipulation   let me void it   rip
      back your five   thousand mondays
        another
           another

          another

       another an

    other

to be greedy
    for a thousand
        rotations of crescents
  must be a crime in every single
      country of this unworthy mythology

        home

home you

    played puck with sleep you
        twisted the zipper between the tide

& eyelid you
      axolotl emerald unfrozen

        pond you order

   ninety more july mornings

      greedy for candy

     for canopus

  like me

you told me to dance so I danced

for our departed mad kin

claws of spool   eyelids of bookmarks

we must have passed   each other

in the hallways of the underworld   a loom hums

more pickle than politics   pluck out each stem

chrysanthemum flock steaming   in other news: downpour

in other butter: suction cups   in other scrabble: three

-star restaurant   you grabbed me more   or less

one lunar calendar apart   the biggest bowl of bath

unrecoverable penny dreadfuls   roof of the word oneiric

sealed with   dorm room dishwater   your nickname

echolalia   my knack   make a wish

stamp a lash   against the papers

(on which they described you)   deferred

echolalia   each should   ereararmdotcollarwingleg

I slant them for you

like a friend would

Carol-Anne

I like being able to make up stories about us.
    —Anthony Sutton, "List of Lies"

§ Ours was a friendship without judgement.

Tell me how easy it was to pick
me over Crystal. How you weren't embarrassed
of my freckles, orange like expired SunnyD. Pale white
three-bedroom bilge *so* seaside trailer, submerged burb
somewhere to park across. Plucked out issues
of *Cosmo* till corner stores caught on our wings.
To collage a childhood until it fell.

You picked it right back.

You were 9-year-old tears or maybe I was.
I was 10-year-old backstabs or maybe you were.
You had a crush on Pat, on Miracle. Chinese big 2
or Shanghainese Chess—you taught me to play

both sides of the table. 3D-printed kid fingers
clawing for carpet, frozen from birth
-day juice ice picks. I applied
Kraft Singles lip gloss on everything I told you about me[1].

We didn't pick at each other when no one was around.

---

[1]   no one was around.

43

§ You didn't succumb.

I smelled safe. I drew flowers on you with expired makeup.
I set fire to your black hair with my red. Muffy
the redhead, Francine without the drumsticks.
We played pretend, tore off our play clothes.

Fire-red pencil-skirted   twenties
Magnetic-sneaker-to-soccer-balled-up   thirties

       barbie vows   barbie vows   barbie vows

Each's peaches. One couldn't tell the other that she

        really[2] really[3] really[4] really[5] really[6] *really*[7]

---

[2] The imaginary house you built with your shoe. The name you gave
your yellow bedroom. The crack in the door and the one-eyed monster.
The itch of your undergarments when you slept, so you took them off.

[3] All things considered, the fact that you ate, for a brief time, on a sheet
of plastic on the floor didn't faze you. What did was as more and more
furniture came into the apartment, there was less and less room to play
with them. The Safeway bears didn't know how to fight the gentrification
of their home or protest the giant new girl who shuffled up into their
lives. There were no hearings they could attend, no public squares.
Unless the gravity.

[4] *if i'm not allowed to miss you then i don't miss you goodbye*

[5] I read about Wulumuqi Road, wondered if you were.

[6]

[7] Today, you believe in every freckle of yourself.

recovery 是

buzzword the coroner picks to accept applications for
perfection(except all you know how to do is burn yourself
up(remember when you were twelve and you wrote yourself out
the tunnel(except you couldn't ride(yourself(of the ridding(you
remain four(as stubborn as ever(how long have you been
hiding(that quiet husk(what they taught you(the kitchen where
she smiled(the park where he fell(everything is small(but you
aren't anymore

))))))

then you put missing them in your calendar

after tax season you stare at the gingko leaf lines of your excel
sheet. long bridges dull linger of lullabies. until. you pause at each
last lantern lit desk doorknob dusk grip laptop foxglove-covered
drawer. open it to sort through documents you were too tired to
sort through last winter. return to each drawstring/word dock/
sticky note: another year, gone. smoke is song-shadow, milk candle
rehearsal. you light things up to shimmer chimney what they'll say
when they hear you. you light things up till your steps are in step
with theirs through history's afterword.

you may not understand now / a 日後 blade of grass

in relation to your dahlias are you 31.1%

a citizen journalist 5.8%

a government agent 5.8%

a start up CEO **57.3%**

a sprig of anguish

picture/sque

in relation to your spell fires are you

an overworked programmer

striking Amazon employees 3.7%

suddenly soft 11%

composting oranges 35.4%

50% are you

in relation to your recipes are you **37.8%**

sea foam 20.7%

a pomegranate stem 26.8%

a guillotine 14.6%

a retired makeup artist

how to choose

if you leave your chosen family does it

mean you have not yet learned how to

choose how to distinguish sickly sweet

marshmallow walls from sturdy pines how

to identify fresh cuts from shadow-stitch

lines how to be a succulent inside

a basement kitchen window how to wilt

gracefully (you did not do anything

gracefully) starburst of mold spores

face morphing into an eyeball window

canopy slow drips with pretend(tend

being your own family

in the plastic reusable boba boy bottle you got from
kerrisdale are two sunflowers who have decided to
become best friends: the nervous tick of your eye
no match for the small taut string looped inside
grandfather's second hand: can't beg against this
already: the true state of diaspora merely an imagined
distance between the epicentre & nowhere:

your four spines nauseate / hurl you inside the corner
of the clock waist your mouth / folded into a broken
crane / tilt your ears through / a string clip strike-slip
/ furniture parts / bump against your neck / you won't
have time left to read the horoscopes /

/ you still hover / over the deaths of those sunflowers
/ did you put enough water in the bottle why / did you
let the budgies stay out in the winter / the suburbs are
a laboratory of failed post-cold war social theories you
want / to sit out in the sun like those giant blooms /
dream of a still yellow now which crumbles / all you
want to do is to squeeze it shut / remain

it won't taste good: floors scrubbed fourteen times but
no slippers to kiss them: spices just sit there: reminder of
a failed school project: a proposal cracked inside brittle
wood: your mayonnaise frowns like

    ice cream inside compost

petals drop, wither. friends that got the best of each
other. collect the pieces as fast as you could. plop your
eye inside bottle. flatten your chest inside the longcase
to make up for the mayonnaise. as small as possible.

Azure Road

your parents aren't ping-pong
   tables, a platter of paranoias,
or the pinyin for *I need to poo.*
   they are just people.

vomiting out carrot cubes:
   your first lesson
in boundary-setting.
   duoduoba animorphs

   into promising
you won't speak
   to them again.
an idiom fathers a child

called memorization
    who kicks mother
(repetition), tries to run away.
    forgets *weishenme*.

you do not family good
    is an idiom you made up
to protect yourself
    from little miss

disappointment. behind her, a dog
    putters across the long carpeted
corridor, only responds to *why continue*.
    stay is not a command. offer

yourself cul-de-sac questions: if they do
    not want you. do you good enough
good enough. an upturned bag
    emptying *perhaps you*

still hope. that someday
    someone will scoop you
up. *all this was a dream, a test.*
    you are not a pottery-wheel's

lump of regret. Raymond
    lost the election that year
but you are not Raymond. you do not
    need to win to live.

forgiving yourself in october
for november mistakes

...get up. The most beautiful part of your body
is where it's headed.
    —Ocean Vuong, "Someday I'll Love Ocean Vuong"

so this is a three-tissue wonton: your teacher tries squeezing out gummy worms from a marble pillar: gloves sewed into crustacean pores: what you don't know you're missing will egg you to hurt: you want to hit everyone trick everyone: only way to shake it is to refuse to fake it: being born kind is a white upper middle class fantasy: that extra five bucks will buy you a heavier boot: it will take millennia to melt the muscle: which ancestor is buried beneath the brine-bowl water plant: if you burn money for them there would you explode too: would Jia Zhangke have made a three-act film of your cousin & your auntie: would their lives be a symphony: the debt he owes her: the debt we owe them aren't called remittances anymore: would you have helped with the lighting or copy-edited the script: would you have clung

I'll Dial Your Number

5

You offer to run him over with your wheelchair. I come to you deceived and smelling of fish oil. You pat my back with your hospital-gown grin. It's so soft I cackle. I cough him out at the rate of decomposing newspapers. Our incense joints speak mutually unintelligible languages. They are our grandmothers' curse words. Two pencils of smoke, two dialects of viral particles. You help me pull out each poisoned seaweed, call it detox. You've never been surer of anything in your life.

My Earth and Ocean Science textbook quotes a west coast city mayor saying,

Citizens should run to higher ground in case of tsunami—run and save yourself first, leave the old and disabled behind.

4

Meeting question: *If you were a kind of medicine, which would you be?* Each time I say pipagao because you gave me ninjiom once in class, that year when my back shook from losing so much to the walls. More than a decade later I am still being remade into the leaves, pit, and fires of loquat. When I rub my face against its orange skin I smell the humidity of the classroom drenched in spring. Something so faint, then six—those gigantic bronze statues of pigeons in Nanjing, triumph of the 70s, alarmed and fascinated you. Our bodies already feel the change. Poking this archive of birds is the game we play together.

3

Our shoebox cluster storage garage is a wok, saucepan, and congee pot fighting for space on the stove. The dishes crowd loudly, complaining about the broken elevator. A plastic spoon writes a passive aggressive note about the wet towels dripping down into her balcony. Napkins twinge with panic. You tell me about the automatic gates that slice off a finger, just a finger, at a time. Waffles in the fridge, only sagging a little. When we crackle and boil, it'll be the pacific that heard us laugh first. I say, under my breath, but loud enough for you to hear, *Fight for those who fight for you.*

2

Your earrings are urgent. My screams don't turn me into a bulletin board case study. You grab the first cab over. I offer you cookies and tea twenty times. Somewhere beneath this bunk bed dampness I chew deserve and grace, swallow them dry.

I'll dial your number. I'll feed your cat. I'll feed your stuffed animals. I'll give you back the water, skip rope around the hurricane. Won't say anything about the rain. On one side of the mist is a clamp of cages. On the other side is. I'm not leaving you behind.

haw flakes, not firecrackers

about anima
ls buying storie
telling I when was
five that firecracke
he singing flakes fi
at one duck we'd cl
ugh the burst abou
ahome our mothe
story by that unashar
ck cassette then on the t
ape for the table we wer
quality of remembering (
o of a video it wasn't one
tearsout she the texture of place sec
five-year-old clothes fabric like firecra
ing which means how xiaoxiong do no
thorn dr   eamt square of the village about every
tle animal each got its turn in the dark blue orange lil
r coming back when I was five I was   telling stories
that one song about how we'd burst through the doors a c
's home intact unashamed she filmed me reciting that sto
ssette back then I ripped out black seaweed from the tape
e blue green hue either the quality of remembering or the c
there this video of a video of a video in which her handling
secret place below overpowering the texture of clothes the f
atched and scratched while telling the story how congming
whoever designed the cylindric paper container for haw tho
village square where everyone's gathered every little anima
orange got its turn to recite like me the steps for going to th
ions for lighting up haw flakes let them

crackle

scratch the night

60

thro
oy abreast to
e filmed intact
n word exactly ba
n delicate multiplications t
hue the green either store the
ht to buy anotherthere this vide
its disgust which noise handling
to the over below texture of the put up with
edandscratched telling the story while she is congm
ainer paper designed whoever flakes cylindric for haw
h the clev ershape gathered every little accounted for lit
steps for going to the market home then instructions fo
ving firecrackers finding haw flakes at the market singing
our hands   a baby on   our breast returning to mother
h word exactly   the order on the audio tape ca
ions table we   went to the store with the pal
uy another kin   d of remembering it wasn't
guts disgust   shooting from car to the
o with fabric li   ke firecrackers she scr
n means do not   handle me
ming about the warm   th of the
ery clever shape in the da rk blue
ing back home the instr   ucti

cker

latewood

                                        losing thumbtacks
                                    losing stanzas
                                losing roof tiles
                            losing fish scales
                        losing pebbles
                    losing latewood   and even
                        losing
                    the moon
        so   pumpkin pie
                        goodbye to   earlier drafts
        of   yourself each night
                                        dayspring with purpled
            ready   to waylay   her   as she sprang th
                            not her   you   lost b

            you
        loose change   stretching
                                                        not a w
                                    but a mother
            existence at the end   of an assembly lin

                                                flushed away
                    that has decided—*how dare she!*—to replac

                    as though dry metallic branches could ever
                                lullaby enough
                                    like clouds lose the

                                                        water-th
            until the bottom of   your   barrel is
                            lost things in a forgotten pocke
        of
            still

                    like
          like
        like
    like
like

        her   ,

        you couldn't   say

                    you refused, hugging curtains of
rs
ie door
      time   not a poem

ost but   the times
              like gorge-sized pouches   of
                    memory   w i d e
    bottle gone
                        hurling away a milk-jug
l   and a bucket   and a bicycle yelling
                    not innocence
              but an umbrella
with the trunk of a tree
      that has long   stopped   sobbing
arm
                        to not let her slip away
in   like there is no difference between the first
 or last   you couldn't hold onto

            the coffee burning your feet
        humble with the rings and shadows

lewy
            others

rewriting the last act of *Mountains May Depart*

Dad loses   wayward Dollar   only dolor   daughter

-son   donates desperate   it's dial-up   Dad

    who left   Fenyang behind this

    once upon a time   love of his life   purpose

      in a wedding suit CD player   exploding

    dynamite   yesterday's

blasted ice   Dad loves his guns but has no enemies

    to shoot at   the absence

ni shenme shihou hui jia

    of an enemy makes his castle wayward

mingtian bu fan dui   raising

waywardness curves Jia's tone   disapproving telephone

    cords   misaligned

Don't be alarmed   I'm glad there was no murder-
suicide   this is not a movie
where anything happens   reviewers find that blood
matters   less than melodrama   two steamers delivered
      meiyou di nayou ni   wolfed down like deer
                                                            It is impossible

to grow up   in a home with grief   trimmed off like a lawn
and not taste familiar   contours of   *tsing oh ka-go*
muffled syllables   buried   beneath   *weh-ling pi-fŏng ziang oh*
        a shirt thrown up   atop the roof   not feign surprise
meiyou wo nayou wo   not trace her outline   across the map of Phonemica

It is impossible

else wrong   Dollar's lack

in the back of your throat

and while Jia gets everything

Dollar doesn't get to visit mother

is just that Dad yelled   Dollar remembers the stings of

"Who cares?"   that flinch too

diamiuhmiuh

zouba

treasure   train   ride

seed that stays

to lose so much so quickly

it's true

of sentimentality in my version

too many times

her scolds

remembers the car ride

remembers the hum of a slow

ni jia liuliu de ku'er

every wayward bygone detail

man enough

my rough / hands my / delinquent's smile my /
   silverware temper my /
        massage chair choked /   with rough /
maps of afternoon / americanos
              like / dried heptapod blood /
   clot in menstrual brake /   fluid a tempo / beating /
the light out / of sound /
              this could be the landing point
    of some story about time or being /
     awake & / taught   how to work
the stubborn / hoops or hide / inside basketball skins
   & somehow wonder if / i wasn't man
              enough for a father / whose crab
-legged brother had crawled /
             those rice-field million days asleep /
before leaving we / suppose / only me
             some stranger

who waited & waited / & waited
   until   sunrise to be / someone /
                that was more than mist /
    beyond a drowned
       friend the banned bark-
           branch guns / the grave of kittens / or
    say / how can you
gravel / these village & minor
       mischiefs / thank my reliable
   man memory / my mulch   fished-dry
       tape recorder
        & suddenly i

am monster / whose real /
home a jail cell & real father /
a judge / penned letter /
grading my birth

certificate for robot / poised in / ready-position / to
leave & carve / away a hole this / wooden toilet eats /
unanswered messages / so if i   could be
your ghost / who lives /

between the / stalls & breathes / in your water or
hisses violent /
brushstrokes of a strong /
& weak / hand then / tell me that

perfect / daughter is man enough / to bear
this stone in a lung
of bobby pins / tell me in your language
so even crab / brother /
and stray unsuspecting /
cats would understand

tulle

sister the world   its cannibal
grief
in your sheared hair
the m u s i c will hear you
—Cynthia Dewi Oka, "to altar"

carry a handmade
zither, like necromancer
   cradling a coffin.

  their plank of tongue writhes
against a made-up language
   for living, then dyes

  a clasp of braided
branches, wiry stitches of
   gingko leaves. gather us

  up: moth, grandmother,
child. pierced with frosted windows,
   blurry from growth. sharp

  black strokes like boats cling
to gun-painted borders. how
   glad I am to be

  alone like this. leap
away from war through steam. spin
   tulle from the smiling

  guzheng, pluck strings of
willow—*Lateralus* in
   another language

line wreckage of wharves,
airports, mouths. the whole river's
here waiting for me.

the shadows of those
who never left my side watch
as I drink them up.

they tell me a dream
is the translation of rot
for the curious

breath of trees, faithful
& wind-shaped. a spiral cord
communion. they

tell me my skin shell
is translucent, a foggy
skylight of spiders

tapping another
artist's oars. this is how I
whisk old things into

now. hands falter through
tulle, caught in a hidden loop,
a spiral cord of trees.

Catalogue of Tearing

dewy decimal isn't a system

of organization but a unit

of water open the library

in refractions ribs of you a cage

a flight of cormorants   *Brittle*

that summer I met you   by brittle

publication date: 2013   a hard vowel

a hard life   ask me a question

what is the stinkiest chemical

what kind of crying

are you looking for

welcome   condensed catacomb

on this floor the spines are soft

a visitor cranks each movable shelf

sink forks to bilge-bottom   locate each

feathery karyotype   careful not to crush

each sweet ROM

oven-hot sweet potato

the moon was pregnant. blushing pink pearl
shifting bottles gather frolic, not anxious. blushes
from knowing sieves of our smiles. mouths are bowls, are
feasts, are watching it all happen. bowls can talk back,
hold the broken water, turn into a hand, a needle, a magic
spell to sew the river back together. i have seen

the soldiers before they come. they wear different uniforms.
they run with machine gun signs: "we protest life,"
"we hate our own breath," "we hate our mother." faces
trained not to twitch when we ask them to join us. cheekily,
i say, "i hope your children abandon you." we will.

the moon is a huge flirt. i text her on lex. tell her i'm
here. say, *why can't i go to the water?* she teases me.
tells me to wait until i'm ready. *don't worry, you'll know.*
charcoal smolders. the water is an archive of dreams.
is a sestina oracle. is a together line brake. is
the children
            of our children
                        of our children

The Organization

in relation to your orbit are you

a couple's first fight — **33.8%**

a brand new motorbike — 8.8%

a wreath of regret — 30.9%

a loyal bottle collector — 26.5%

in relation to your rolling pin are you

a life hack — 5.1%

grey socks in sandals — 21.8%

suppressed grief — **55.1%**

SUV headlights — 17.9%

in relation to your fingernails are you

an emoji sent in error — **32.1%**

sparkly pom poms — 3.8%

posthumous autobiography — **32.1%**

a confused tadpole — **32.1%**

WHEN YOU JOINED
the INDUSTRY of Caring, it was
to *take* a Vacation from
the INDUSTRY *of* LANGUAGE

Here Language WAS a
grocery bag to hold
OUR hands as they
shouldered surplus Care .

The carrying Of Good
do ing in a gro·cer·y bag
meant you of·ten
THOUGHT about the grey
car with its black
trunk . There

are NO ▢ vacations
on this ski resort
WITH tarp S
made of grocery
bags *and* hands.

Bags chose hands
that were ALREADY
weary and hands
that rarely worried

equally . *they* were
fair. Eventually
you learned
your hand

exhaust

yesterday, there was a
fire truck that took too
long to get to the other
side of the bridge.

I took a long, long time
to get to the bathroom
at 3:12am. I churned out
another month of chores
except you weren't there

to see it. I keep up hope
as a beach ball who wandered
across the road up the alley
where a maroon couch
sank deeper into a dizzy

sigh. the sky above your
morning was made of algae.
I tried being wrong like
a dress. I tried leaving
afraid behind like a deserted

tail that no longer served
my generation. weather
no longer made sense without
you. I'm tired of the dust on
top of the fridge. I reached

out the window of the truck
like I could still touch your
face. I needed to be right
back then. how lonely
that was for you.

The host has disabled attendee chat

Dear attendee,

Now that you've given me the role of host,
    of speaker, I ask you if I'm allowed
to open the spine of my neck, reveal

a single barcode of leaves & blue sky
projected on bare knuckles of a self
    -effacing question—the size of a split
hulusi (burned on it, my first name), pry
    this punctuation apart with an itch
in the eyebrow that reminds me of an
    other's touch. I flip-flop the perspective
until the frame cuts fast to you, wilting,
    flat, sweaty on the grass-lemon section
of your trimmed page-hedges. I hugged my friends
    on my 93rd birthday. They were not
perfect hugs so I want to try again.
    Sweet attendee, I have nothing to say
about the breath. The miracle of our
    automatic nervous systems belongs
to whoever beyond us we believe
    in more than our grandmothers. For some there
is no such thing. I take your hand & guide
    you through the screen. Linger here where it hurts
the most. The apartment where she raised me,
    the one with the turquoise door—no, the one
with the green gate… no, I don't know. I won't
    run away with memory, fold the loose
40 bucks in my pocket. Then try to
    unsmell construction sawdust in flecks of
eggs folded in a worker's fried rice. If
    you're bored, you're entitled to a refund.
Attendee, you who have not tuned me out:
    Why did you join this meeting? What were you
expecting? The country changed so fast. We
    grew twice as big as Shanghai Tower. Defer

to your opinion—does this building
    meet zoning code? The 80s called & she
wants her one chance back. Please. Do not let them

rewrite history: [this portion of the
webinar skipped to preserve the contents
        of a jar, an airtight dignity] what
the cops couldn't get to first. Then who was
        responsible for the great leap forward?
It would be a question she scrubbed herself
        too many times to answer. Goddamnit,
you look uncomfortable. Since we can't switch
        lips on this dimension, how about I
leave you with a volta about hunger?

is it literature or deforestation?

national chiropractor bench
national unwritten existentialist philosophy pape
national pretend I don't miss you
national dried squid packet
national dusty badminton racket
national underwear folding techniques
national fluoride-free toothpaste
national crocheted dishcloth
national paper cut
national broken tweezer
national somatic flashback
national *In the Mood for Love*
national acrylic picture frame
national breathing technique
national teasing that borders on hazing
national ripped curtains
national finger-pointing
investment
foreign navel-gazing
foreign flapping curtains
foreign teasing that borders on hazing
foreign breathing technique
foreign acrylic picture frame
foreign *The Stories We Tell*
foreign panic attacks
foreign lactose pills
foreign wood sliver
foreign knitted bucket hat
foreign fluoride-free toothpaste
foreign forgetting you left the stove on
foreign dusty badminton racket
foreign preserved olives
foreign admit I still miss you
foreign confession scrawled with ineligible handwriting
foreign chiropractor bench

you imagine her in the faces of others: you see the mogui of race in the crowds of this too-Asian campus: so you emptied yourself of what they saw as competition: remaining useless so you no longer needed needing: years later he will Gwen Stefani another sidekick: she will have the same name as you: will get another chance to pay respects: stilling a compass of coincidence: had a knife fight in the Uwajimaya parking lot: not a shell (not a shell): you belong to shoe polish: you belong to gavel polish: goodbye 2014: your legs froze: your throat thawed: you ripped up their contract: refused to take hush money: god/dess of mercy smiling through the paragraphs: ghosts: historians: hesitations: scrawled hi: hello: the caramel salt sting: sigh: won't be long now

home economics

what would you call a peach

with several new bite marks?

throw a hook as sharp as chili

appetizer into that tourist Etch

A Sketch. you'd rather be steam.

one day I'll leave this town

hitting pavement sideways(candle this wax(delivery milquetoast
severance(bread waiver sigh scribble(frozen(for 23 years—
(cumming on green bedsheets (your neck pin casualty clause
(graffitied his copy(electric whirling counter(tequila eyes meeting
(tiny hats lipsticker unglue(unglue lipsticker hat tiny meeting
eyes tequila(counter whirling electric copy)his graffitied clause
casualty pin)neck your bedsheets)green)on cumming years 23—
for scribble)sigh)waiver bread severance milquetoast delivery)wax
this candleside ways)pavement hitting))))))))))

one day this town will leave me

autist roams the strip malls of 3 road

lands in blenz / grips

drops on   some start-up guy   dream board / aircrafts

operation / no supervisor   except   the one /

cider   mitten / clasps   her meridian

how   tomorrows

are like temples /

lights / this booth   / all hers   how

in

boston /   this make-believe reunion

estranged cousins   sprinkling our lives on

pizza / /

to find them   / while languishing

is it selfish to dance /   on the outer

conversation   like horizon

*still **I** dream of*

craters of twenty / eaves

hover over   another earth /   some other jia

trauma   wonder   glued to her ass /   apple

fridge instructions   /   how to overhear

crept across her

brow / strip malls

praying to caffeine and wi-fi / 3am

sizzle the third descent   / granola cement

won't find her   twice /

a stranger /   is it hypocritical to want

in the secret barrier of being   / unreachable

eardrum of another/s

/ like the man in dirty vegas/   /   days go by   /

still I dream of

85

1-Star Motel in Yr San Junipero Heart

X is a Japanophile/Canucks fan.
      Being his second (third?) Chinese something
            or other was like picking chewed-up bones

with yr teeth—a close-up scene of sea soup
      we slurped from inside a trench kitchen. Man,
            I still love that guy though. Every friend's all,

You dodged a bullet made of normie/weeb.
      But I'm like. Let me have this one. Nothing
            is quite the same as yr early twenties:

we drank milkshake & didn't hold hands. Phones
      connect our spooled blood vessels—DMs keep
            our fingers tied like rubber promise rings

we wouldn't wear. Train passes Hangzhou. Plenty
      of times I would lie there, synapse a loop
            of *if only*. I jumped into men's beds

to survive. I could tell him now, *Thank you*
      for this temporary home. Why I'm not
            mad, why I won't excavate meaning from

our clumsy reticent bodies is cuz
      What does this remind you of? is boring.
            I'll psychoanalyze myself later.

After poking him with my hair clip (knot
      after knot of tomorrow in our heads),
            I blocked him on FB but not on Skype.

Tomorrow is an impulsive fog. Clones
    of bad men were everywhere. So were sneers
        behind each queer *shhh, you're safe with me.*

X wasn't bad. X will forever be
    my sweet bare minimum against whom all
        others will be judged. Wait, hold on. Will you

hold me like he once did. Will you hold me
    like lovers in San Junipero. Fall
        sizzled, sighed. My elephant-feet crater

heart stomped out recollections of mirrors,
    twisting our faces into denying
        their stink bug jarred fates. Won't let you wipe

my crater-crow umbrella feet dry. Dupe
    me into staying until the years fuzz
        & fade. I know it's not twenty

sixteen anymore. A fusion of gems
    is all I want to curl myself inside.
        Let this become an experience you

can't market as blankets. I wade beside
    you inside an overflowing Cháng Thames,
        a dam of seconds but not second best.

Inside this one-heart motel of autumn
    stars are raptors of mourning. Kept the rest
        of these memories a secret. Help me

conceal parts that healed her shrapnel wounds. Sing
    the OST until you believe in
        yourself again. Silly, we're not alone.

How Pine Needles Ate the Subaru

1   Squeegee away the daze

2   Windshield wiper the atrium

> pour pine-needle creamer
> into teacup where I end you begin
> the trunk our tangled hairs dried
> valve carcass-shell museums two
> sets of grandparents I want to take
> care of someone each time

3   Flip car over left lung

> *Take out the rhododendron*
> *Fold lonely into drawers*
> *Cut out potato sprouts*
> *Vacuum the rejection*
> *Fill the hot water bag*
> *Hang me on the balcony*
> *Kiss polyester*

4   Crumple the ventricle highway

> my femur cannot be found

5   Sew chambers out of chicken skin

> you combed through my scratched
> CDs rustled me apart lifted me
> from the nose pad your driving glasses
> used me to wipe off the laminate
> calcareous soil where I fend for myself

6   Wrench apart shoulders

            it's only then it's only then

7   Break clavicle spoons

            drive away from overdue
            notice roads frayed into exhaust
            lumber fry engines expire

8   Chew on the vessels

            release my pine-needle hands

9   Let shoots fall

            Pressed flower bookmark
            Baked potato skins
            Dew-filled cones
            Belly warm & full

10   Exhale the calluses that host them

            relearn what it means
            for the sky to hold me

Fiddling with My Chew Toy Strolling Across
Matthew Wong's *River at Night* (2018)

Smith also noted that none of the works were for sale. There was no talk of the artist's market. But collectors with an eye toward speculation can only be held back on moral grounds for so long. By February, I got a text from an advisor asking where one could get a Matthew Wong, saying, "I have a client who's going to have a heart attack if he doesn't get one—he will pay, like, any price."

—Nate Freeman, May 7, 2020, "Wet Paint: Jordan Wolfson
Really Hates the New Jordan Wolfson Documentary,
a New York Gallery Defies Quarantine,
& More Juicy Art-World Gossip," *Artnet News*

$1400

By December I'd been, as Gen Z TikTokers say, wanting
        to unalive myself for 3-months straight. Let me
approximate a name for (azn woman) (Vancity arts) community
        (who took her own life) or (nobody tells me) taunting.

$5000

        Google turns up Tkaronto-born autist, grew up
in Hong Kong. After his death, Matthew's art sold
        for tens of thousands of not getting to grow old.
Wishfully I mumble, "Can't exploit me if I'm a fuck-up."

$6800

One theory: The US State Department trained
        HK police to tear through the harbour while auctioneers
salivated for paint. Nostalgic for CIA-backed Pollock, gears
        of the Art World cranked out a beautiful mind, chained

$12K

hands raw to the steel of old money, new money, whiteness.
       It's scary out there, and not for the reasons you think. O
Matthew. Why did the artist steal the person? Why did you go
       so soon? Daydreaming suicide offers me escape; lightness.

$51K

       There's nowhere on earth to escape to.
In "River at Night," the river is a road and the trees sway
and the flowers and leaves are boxes. How do I stay
       treading in boxes. Or wait until you

$400K

come back. Invite you over for lunch. (Tea's ready.)
       Let us be boring and unextraordinary. Can I also sit here
in the deep end? Snip photographs, uncoordinated, near.
       What hue is living. Where do we eddy.

$3 million

I look at your art for free/at the rate of monthly Internet. Graze
       each screen-stroke with haughty hands. Gust of oils, like
the quiet. Chirps of morning, or violence. I like
       painting weird faces. I don't want to sell my art. The maze

$50 million

       of industry makes me develop an anxious tic where
I say I'm a bad person like Beetlejuice, a sticky curse.
       Back in 2015 a man who wrote Python verse
tells me I'm a good. Dare I believe him; paint a world I can bear.

blaring "Fly Like A Bird" across the Yellowhead Highway

what were
you doing   when the world
dipped deep   & the mountain   shivered
like   a lost pen   beneath   a desk
so   unattended to   you felt her   unearned collapse
tremor of elbow   wide jab   car doors
a canyon receipt   that's when you fell   butterfly wind   beating
silver   toyota   run   away

into a highway
broken CD   dangling   tagged along by   the ankles

trying to catch   a fruit fly   trap it

with your bare   hands   first   forgetting of

buzzing   unaware   you had ten toes   smother

of curiosity   you cut   with your entire body

someone else's   so six   so small   did not smell pity

musty fried rice karaoke   apartment under   construction

like all smotherings   a part of you still   inched

a little bird   toward carbon   monoxide smog   horn announcement

notes   you held up   a clay bird   you held up   little red flags
said   *look look*   *country*
i've been good   *i've been so so good*
as if that's all you gave   as if you didn't break it
with your
bare hands

Walking into the Ocean

My obligation to the earth is simpler than the flimsy contract of a collapsed toy-ship factory. How long fish would live if no longer fugitive to keel, kellick, and angry boom-chain? Injecting Botox into the water. Workers of our county must have looked forward to the coolness of soil when they drowned. The last of their incense-breaths fleeing Pender Street, home between ashy pages of quiet night and negligent morning. That portion of motherland christened "Oriental Hawaii." Which part did you name me after? I watch as you twist anchor lines with steaming red sausage. Squeeze blood from wet towel.

I get it all mixed up—water from sausage oil, sunspots from badges of living. Tell me the difference between my bones and the bones of whale shark. This nuclear explosion paints brush strokes like iron filings. My ghost grips my neck until

I can breathe again. The ocean knows too much, would reject me too. The pomelo at the corner of our fridge, untouched for months. Face torn up like sausage skin. Roof of my mouth softens, mistaken for glue. The ocean is a fable, seaweed stuck between front teeth. If we lay our hides side by side, which of us has more scales? And after all of it: *I ride nekton back to before I walked. To find my baby-body fed.* A warmth I have betrayed has betrayed me.

Who can say if this daydream is more walking than water. More empty swing than drop. Unwound spool and a jar of kitchen grease, honeying frozen flies. Somehow the tea is still cold; like you have forgotten who I am. What would you do if I could become a worm wedged in this subduction zone boundary between us, waking up to everything, gone? The ocean is not a feeling, not a child, not a mother, not a worker, not a word. She is quaking, spinning, ablaze. An oven of unfinished business. A forehead. Still learning from contours of glass—like we are.

in relation to your dahlias are you

___ a citizen journalist

___ a government agent

___ a start-up CEO

___ a sprig of anguish

in relation to your spell fires are you

___ an overworked programmer

___ striking Amazon employees

___ suddenly soft

___ composting oranges

in relation to your recipes are you

___ sea foam

___ a pomegranate stem

___ a guillotine

___ a retired makeup artist

ECHOLALIA AS A SECOND LANGUAGE

in relation to your hesitation are you

___ a shudder

___ triple A batteries

___ striped shoelaces

___ a field of corns

i wish i could write poems
after Desirée Dawson

about quiet lakes roads that wound & wound
    until you saw a bear slip your crush's hands into a clasp
    the horizon melted smile of your eyes stayed it wanted to stay

about lilac baubles near Azure you beamed
    bouncy chorus pigtail gel penned candies on Halloween
    soft with cherry scents eye makeup joy without reservation

about galloping galaxy
    blankets of dots that waved when you saw them
    don't worry I'm here, I'm here

about binge-watching *Arthur* until 4am shifting
    sandbox clumsy knees turning to shake pebble tears around
    & around the others can't see you

about wiping away
    memories (did you know?) a new poem is a counter
    that no longer has nightmares

made of spicy Indomie noodles
    & fried rice repetitions that somehow
    (I don't know how) got the rent paid

like your sheepish
    I'm sorry that rainy autumn evening took away
    your crayons marbles Oreos budgies even the worms (!!!)

about How to Be Good but your sixth-grade teacher said *oh no*
    you can't do that when you flipped through the little red
    Testament at silent reading that November

about the papery red boxes at yeye nainai's
    roasted chicken by the big big grave it happened
  to smack your name right dab in the middle

about Minoru Park herons who mimicked
    the love life of old ones
  all summer all winter the lifelong watchers of lunes

about monkey bar hands that burned & bloomed
    against the new black Billabong hoodie the cool girl
  was mad I wore on the same Wednesday as she did

I wish I could write poems where the poem's alive marched
    into my apartment to slap the coffee table let in a cat
  with a wide wide mouth I took lots & lots of photos

shouted *it's the next ice age!* & the mirror in the bathroom
    whispered *I love you I love you*
  where the poems are asleep

during nap time at preschool with one stanza open
    watched & wondered what it would be like to be taller
  oh taller than a stanza one day one day

notes app apology

after Danez Smith

Dare Me,

every time u try 2 apologize & acknowledge the things u did
when u were hurt u burst into tears & stop yrself from doing
it. y?? u ask yr best friend like an angry fly buzzing thru the
phone—he tells u we r simultaneously all the ages we once
were inside & not just our adult bodies. 2 apologize 4 this is
also 2 apologize 2 the kid u punched when u were seven & 2
apologize 2 yr elementary school bully even tho that was a
hecked up thing she did with the group of other kids

in the fishbowl. they tore up yr internal netspeak like they
would at every misspoken 'th' if u hadn't torpedoed yr
mouth thru g-force & relativity each intentional misspelling
a hazard against catapult piled on top of u on xanga told
u 2 go back 2 HK even tho u r not from HK but some of
their parents were. who taught them this lash-out grief. who
taught u. everyl's heard a dialect or 2 of that 1. 2 get back to

The Apology though: it isn't Fair 2 ask anyl else 2 reParent
u if they know adult u & had nothing to do with happened to
u when u were eleven. people were responsible tho. ask the
Grandmothers. u thought North American Protestantism
was like Daoism & that was the only mistake u made. an
apology can't carry an elephant or a hippocampus. we aren't
born 2 stay clean. fists fresh apricots then. little jane, little
jane. u can delete this if u want. no one needs to forgive u.

i want to know what comes after

You retweeted
Hiromi Goto @hinganai.5h
*How water loves us
unconditionally.*

camera defines rain
    rings in my ears
        on the other side
screen is a fluid birdsong
    small trickle of blight
overused iPhone hologram
    reaches you through sweaty fingerprints
i bought a bangle that looked like the moon
    to feel majestic without touching the rain
you see (me)   it was to make up
    for what i lost
[video description: 16 seconds
  cable news hummingbird feed
    Saturday evening filmed five hours ago
      ]
        a sharp unlikely connection
    green message boxes   delete delete delete
  colour-coded apps   not tea leaves
but here is a mantra: Orangina is
    water tears are water
urine is water   cum stains were once water
    dirt moss   stream made of continuous
      fresh salt
    i ask our Insta-temple
    why wasn't i worth fighting for
      knowing those i grieve can't   won't
    at the frayed edges of condition
        read my question

betrayal

yellow cranes above salt hatch concrete

potty bowls swell their well-worn weapons
feather daggers zip the alabaster night
drip-tie wooden beads IV red strings
who twisted the handle coiled & burning
who scolded their error-ridden triets
the one who couldn't fight him off
the one channeling her uncle's
arrested at 20 in Tiananmen
carrying blue sacks across the yellow country

why did you betray me
if you hadn't betrayed me
why did you betray me

carrying blue sacks across the yellow country
arrested at 20 in Tiananmen
young ones channeling their uncle's
old ones who would fight him off
who licked their arrow-ridden foreheads
who washed the bowstring sharp & coiling
almanac of callouses drip-tie plastic beads
floating esophagus zip the alabaster night
swollen card palm splays their feathers bare

concrete salt hatch yellow cranes above

100 Punchlines to Procrastinate Kicking Your Bucket

Give yourself ten minutes.
Give yourself ten years.
— Kaitlyn Boulding, "Questions to Ask Yourself Before Giving Up"

The most delicious peach
has yet to be devoured. Many persimmons
have yet to sublet your mouth. You don't believe lychees
exist after you're gone (but that's the ego talking). What
hubris to assume you've eaten enough
(or the best!) xiaolongbao! The woman at Sun
Fresh Bakery would wonder where you've gone. Your palate
for BBQ is, at this moment, woefully incomplete. What if
the best bubble tea flavour is out there somewhere?
Many people have yet to try your durian dumplings
(thanks, Tony, for the recipe!). You still need to find
out if there's a fruit dumpling that would be utterly disastrous.

One day you will return to their farm. You promised
to fold H*rper into a dumpling & dip
him in fracking oil. You haven't yet promised to dip
Tr*deau into a dumpling & dip him in LNG sauce. Some local
politicians haven't blocked you yet (uhm
what are you all waiting for?!). There are at least three dozen
acupuncture points she hasn't yet poked. How
will your acupuncturist find out what happened?
Your flesh suit craves watercolour snakes, crayon
fruits, neon leaves, silly faces. One day the sea
will have come back; you will want to smell her salt
body against your skin. So many stickers

have yet to find their surface. There are so many pebbles
who pine for the heat of your palm. There are oceans
of sand you haven't grazed with your fingers. There are many
more deep-sea creatures to fall in love with.
If a week later they find out
how eels have sex, how can you forgive yourself?
Tardigrades would send in a complaint.
The quantum entanglement committee would read the report
instantly, how embarrassing. They will find out
you abandoned a String of Buttons in a mason jar.
You won't be around to submit an appeal, now
that's REALLY embarrassing. The sweetest cat

you've ever met will be sad.
Your other favourite cat will also be sad.
You're madly in love with his dad. Okay, it's more
of a long-standing crush but let's exaggerate
a little here, okay? Wouldn't it be fun
to exaggerate a little while longer. Koalas don't know
how to fight ostriches
& only you have the instructions. To croak
having only tried two vibrators is a great waste.
You'd be so sexy with silver hair. You have no clue
at which pinprick geographic coordinates
you'd like to be buried. Leaving

this earth without having gone stargazing
would be your worst offense. Your lips will crack open
below your final aurora borealis; you won't notice. If

you haven't read the spiritual texts, how can you say
you've figured it all out? There are still so many
more Dionne Brand books to read.
There are still so many little leaves to pocket
& leave alone. There are still so many jelly beans to name.
There are so many more puppies to pet.

There are so many more people to piss off. Someone out there
knows how to touch you, properly.
It will be after you let yourself teach them.
You haven't talked to a lawyer about what to do
about your assets. Who are we kidding?
Better to spend your money on fairy lights. It will take

a while longer to earn six figs in *Virtual Fisher#7036*.
The fish would not be happy
if you didn't get them Wise Bait at level 50. Maybe
at level 50 they'll tell you what Wise Bait is.   You haven't
watched every one of Wong Kar-Wai's film—heresy.
There's enough time on this earth
to watch all of Alanis Obomsawin's films. If you haven't
watched all the movies Lucy Liu has ever appeared in,
what is even the point? It is unacceptable
that you haven't watched all of *Sailor Moon!*
It is unacceptable that you haven't watched
the episode where Mr. Ratburn gets married!

It is unacceptable that you haven't gotten
to the gayest part of *Adventure Time!*
You & Brianna haven't yet co-written that Vancity
Sherlock Holmes adaptation. When the show flops exactly
twenty-one years later you two and everyone else will laugh.
You haven't written that horror story like you promised,
how rude. There are still a hundred hours
of B-roll to edit. There are still a hundred hours
of audio to edit. There are still so many TikTok
videos to snort at. There are so many brooms for you
to shoplift. With which to roll up bad dreams like *Katamari*.
You will get to sweep up alibis so many more times.

There is another moment, another breath.
You simply haven't sung karaoke enough times, darling.
If you're not at your own memorial, how

would everything go as planned? Sorry but it's just not okay
to not have tried ACID at least once.
What?   Dying before Genocide Joe?   What?!
They haven't yet invented a lighter
you can use. Imagine retiring & living somewhere
you can get paint on the floor & there's a slide!
Someone on WeChat can teach you how to speak
Liuhenghua. Someone on WeChat can teach you
how to speak Pujianghua. What kind

of millennial would you be if you've never seen MCR in
concert? One day you'll be the W6RST
in an all-queer azn prog metal band. One day they'll
realize reincarnation is real. You have not
made up your mind about whether this is the right choice
philosophically. You want to be there
when the prisons crumble. The Judge Rotenburg Center
in Canton, Massachusetts is still open. There are things worse
than death, yes, but inside a hole punch
you aren't in danger.   You'd be so cute
having completed your four thousand & sixty-nineth
mental breakdown. What if in 2060: no one

is without/too much.   What if
in 2070: every leaf is a home/space odyssey.
What if tomorrow: you learn how to apologize.
What if they invent a time machine.
What if too late is not part of its programming.
What if you were secretly a magician.
What if they believed you.

There are still so many spices for your tongue to tease.
A few more hours of stimming & you'll feel better.
Just another episode & it's bedtime for real.
A timer cannot go past its battery life.
Waiting & waiting & waiting is part of the process.

Maybe they'll send you another song.
Another meme will make you laugh.
This is not the closure you were searching for.

This is not the peace you were searching for.
This is not the freedom you were searching for.

It would be silly to let them win.

Projections

I sit in what used to be your room look
    out a grinning basement window you

wouldn't let me peer inside the silence of
    this house without the arch

of your stirrup the safety of a pocket knife
    used to cut through time the mitochondria

of clouds of pink promises a room is a suit
    case turned voluptuous & wide

so full of breath so closed with a zipper
    yanked to keep me tucked in a bent

envelope your side pocket didn't notice too
    busy gripping & gripping to keep you high

on my loftiness enough to hold half my rolled
    -up receipts those bad memories

from all the fawns & turtles you skinned
    alive just for them to trundle across the hall

& hiccup at my slippers while every
    one else is thinking about the results of

the election about Greta about the rate
    of snowmelt I slam down a decade of mistakes

just to ask you one last time to let me see
    just let me have this one look inside

Therapy Park

fishing is shadow work we can do it in a steam game

deep seeing of eclipse mirrors blank marks a back

then carries a pearl each scale is two people a balance

that subsides all specificities shadow work is fishing

clams asleep in a groove of nails take me to Therapy Park

where you pull patterns from polka dot mouths i bare

clipped fins to hunting nets isn't exactly love is a shroud

of barley water pointing one serendipitous finger no spatulas

only whiskers i no longer wished to disappear but shadow

work is sunlight a lioness leaves her cubs to claw a highway

cave's trail earth scent parallel universes bouncing off dodgeballs

thank you thank you we are both nuts the squirrels have found

us droplets of moonbeam a laugh after all gives us away

in relation to your poetry are you

grandfather's eyebrows   14.1%

a tight corner   25%

another cavity   29.7%

a will to live on   **31.3%**

queerwork

we found
a droplet of hope
in soil-lined rocks soft
ankle palms mug of some avocado
plant tall & tentative so
bodied then
ready to
learn

to fold
pie-slices of forests
into sculptural breaths
forgiving secrets be-shadowed
& lamp-kissed skin crevice
after crevice faith
of our make
-shift

hand
-drift designs
you tell me my
home is a knife
pleat fold & you are
right & good
in whatever
language
that

is
right
& good
because the
curious & queer
workings of this
makeshift room
is brick walls
crumbling
into bits of
scrap

paper
whiteness
fading into lamp
-shades of mountains
through our eager
so very sore
& eager
hands

Acknowledgements

I am indebted to the care and grace that my loved ones extended me throughout writing *echolalia echolalia*. 謝謝 for holding me when I didn't know how: that, too, is a poem.

Thank you to my editor Phoebe Wang for the generous support and care. Every round of edits felt like a gift, a breeze. Enormous gratitude goes to Cynthia Dewi Oka for guiding me to the centre of the whirlpool that is *echolalia echolalia*. Thank you, Shazia Hafiz Ramji, for the invaluable guidance that helped shape my initial drafts into a book.

I owe the final form of my title to Beni Xiao, one of this book's first readers. Thank you for being an incredible pal and discerning reader.

Tremendous thanks to Kayla Czaga for the meticulous mentorship and attention throughout The Writer's Studio workshops. I owe so much to your care and your class. Thank you Tara Borin, df parizeau, Ashley Hynd, Ping Alexandra, Cecil Hershler, Bre Neufeld, and Janna Walsh for the beautiful time spent with poems.

So much gratitude to Diana Khoi Nguyen for offering me the courage to release this work into the world. To my fellow Tin House Summer Workshop poets Cindy Juyoung Ok, Eddie Angelbello, Gauri Awasthi, Mark Bias, Nicole Homer, Reece Gritzmacher, and Susan Nguyen. I am so honoured our work crossed paths.

To Mallory Tater, Brandi Bird, Selina Boan, and the rest of The Rahila's Ghost Press team: thank you so much for creating the necessary scaffolding for this nascent project through *Leaving Chang'e on Read*.

Alayna Munce and Emma Allain and the rest of the Brick Books team—thank you for the spaciousness you conjured to bring *echolalalia echolalia* to life. This experience feels like a once in a lifetime.

Much love to Warsan Shire for the generous witnessing. To Rita Wong for the movement mentorship. To Annick MacAskill for pointing me in such generative directions. To D.M. Bradford for your spirited support and incisive readership. To Mercedes Eng for ushering me along. To Joy Priest for the permission to play. To Patricia Smith for opening a doorway. To Terese Marie Mailhot for the teachings on truth-telling when both I and the poems needed them. To Cyrée Jarelle Johnson for the precision and encouragement. To Kay Ulanday Barett for the sense of community. To Travis Chi Wing Lau for seeing me. To Alice Wong for welcoming my crip creativity and determination. To Leah Lakshmi Piepzna-Samarasinha your wisdom and perspective. To Tolu Oloruntoba for the quiet offers of care. To Rebecca Salazar for the crip kinship. To Manahil Bandukwala for the ongoing support. To Maneo Mohale for the witnessing. To Xine Yao for the trust. To Nisha Patel for the shared language. To Karlene Harvey for the design input. To T. Liem for believing in my work. To Alex Leslie for the conversations.

shō yamagushiku—for all the voice notes and for witnessing the spirit at the heart of this text, I will always be grateful. Poetry pals for life!

Yilin Wang—thanks so much for the literary friendship and spirited conversations on translation and ethics throughout the years.

Tonye Aganaba, thank you for opening a corner of your home to me. Thank you to Rasha Abdulhadi, for the necessary guidance and perspective on the role of poetry in this hour of the world. Thank you to Joselia Hughes for your presence and kindness. To SF Ho, thank you for being there for me!

I could not have written *echolalia echolalia* without being challenged and cared for alongside a waterfall of thinkers, artists, musicians, care workers, organizers, poets, writers, filmmakers whose work resonated with me, who offered me care, who invited to the front of the room, and who read, shared, and edited my work. Thank you to *ROOM*, *Canthius*, and all the other small literary spaces that welcomed me. To everyone here and more:

Idil Abdillahi, Jordan Abel, Afuwa, Rusaba Alam, Hari Alluri, Amber Dawn, Phanuel Antwi, Manuel Axel Strain, Brit Bachmann, Adèle Barclay, Billy-Ray Belcourt, Serena Lukas Bhandar, Shashi Bhat, Ali Blythe, Dionne Brand, Jody Chan, Ellen Chang-Richardson, Kazumi Chin, Céline Chuang, Jillian Christmas, Haisla Collins, Wayde Compton, Sean Cranbury, Philip Crymble, Dina Del Bucchia, Tania De Rozario, Saima Desai, Junie Désil, Vi An Diep, Farzana Doctor, Cecily Downs, Justin Ducharme, Ivy Edad, Savannah Erasmus, Samah Fadil, Summer Farah, Phebe Ferrer, Jen Ferguson, Raoul Fernandes, Dana Fletcher, Deanna Fong, Richard Fung, Czaerra Galicinao Ucol, Seemi Ghazi, Dionna Griffin-Irons, Guérin, Joy Gyamfi, June Hawthorn, Kevin Andrew Heslop, Bara Hladík, Sandy Ho, Lisa Hofmann-Kuroda, Leah Horlick, Eileen Holowka, Liz Howard, Tiffany Hsiung, Hua Xi, Marcela Huerta, Adrienne Carey Hurley, Chantal James, Kumar Jensen, Jia Zhangke, Aisha Sasha John, Wanda John-Kehewin, Jessica Johns, Raven John, Samantha Jones, Tamara Jong, Joelle Jeffrey, Tyemhimba Jess, Valeen Jules, Petero Kalulé, Alia Kassab, Divya Kaur, Douglas Kearney, Jónína Kirton, EJ Kneifel, Chelene Knight, Rahat Kurd, Lydia Kwa, Holly Lam, Larissa Lai, Laiwan, Grace Lau, Rachel Lau, Christina Lee, Erica Violet Lee, Jen Sookfong Lee, Kathryn 君妍 Gwun-Yeen Lennon, Ian LeTourneau, Carrianne Leung, Catherine Lewis, Toria Liao, Lisa Lieberman, Natalie Lim, Thea Lim, David Ly, Nya Lewis, TL Lewis, Vivian Li, Zefyr Lisowski, Layli Long Soldier, Lucia Lorenzi, Pearl Low, Tin Lorica, Canisia Lubrin, Caleb Luna, Terese Mason Pierre, Wendy Matsumura, Chandra Melting Tallow, Estlin McPhee, Kílila McMath, Vuyokazi Mgoduka, ViNa Nguyễn, Kathryn Mockler, Sarah Munawar, Cassandra Myers, Hasan Namir, Zehra Naqvi, Rhiannon Ng Cheng Hin, Hue Nguyen, Samantha Marie Nock, Arit Nsemo, Chimedum Ohaegbu, Michael Paramo, Rebecca Peng, Marc Perez, M. NourbeSe Philip, Dan Pon, Natasha Ramatour, Dev Ramsawakh, Zofia Rose, Hamza Salha, Cavar

Sarah, Dan Shapiro, Christina Sharpe, Erin Soros, Kevin Spenst, Kara Stanton, Kelsey Stoner, Steffy Tad-y, Hsien Chong Tan, Lea Taranto, Kai Cheng Thom, Chrysanthemum Tran, Lauren Turner, Chimwemwe Undi, Shristi Uprety, Kim Villagante, Fred Wah, Rinaldo Walcott, Isabella Wang, Sanna Wani, Natalie Wee, Casey Wei, Melissa West Morrison, Jaz Whitford, Danielle Wong, Jackie Wong, Florence Yee, Clare Yow, Ava Yunus, Daniel Zomparelli, Jacquelyn Zong-Li Ross.

Nikki, amanda, Tray, Vivian, Sunny, Rabbit, Q, Rach, Shianna, Judah, Odera, Tina, Santi, Brianna, Clair, Ash, Sankofa, Bill, River, Whess, Hue, Y Vy, Cathleen, Siling, Jaxsun, and many others: I'm so happy you are here.

echolalia echolalia was written on the occupied and stolen lands of the xʷməθkʷəy̓əm (Musqueam), Sḵwx̱wú7mesh Úxwumixw (Squamish), səl̓ilw̓ətaʔɬ (Tsleil-Waututh), Kwantlen, q̓íc̓əy̓ (Katzie), Semiahmoo, Tsawwassen, kʷikʷəƛ̓əm (Kwikwetlem), Stó:lō, lək̓ʷəŋən (Lekwungen), Ojibwe, Odawa, Potawatomi, Ho'Chunk, Meskwaki, Sauk, and Miami Nations. Writing is a sacred gift. My work will always be indebted to the caretaker of these lands and to the stolen peoples living here.

Notes

Gratitude to the editors for publishing versions of these poems in *The Capilano Review, The Offing, EVENT, Geist, Thirteen: New Collected Poems from LGBTQI2S Writers in Canada, the 2022 MAU Calendar, Watch Your Head* online and the *Watch Your Head: Writers & Writers Respond to the Climate Crisis* anthology, *Canthius, PRISM international, The Fiddlehead, The Ex-Puritan, AZE journal: Volume 3 Issue 3, ANMLY: Writing Ourselves / Mad, The /tƐmz/ Review, CV2 Magazine: Sick Poetics*, and in the chapbook *Leaving Chang'e on Read* (Rahila's Ghost Press, 2022).

"Reading Practice" follows Otoniya Okot Bitek's call to "sully language, to do whatever we want with it," from the talk "Language, Literature, and Translation: Otoniya Okot Bitek in Conversation with Wangui wa Goro & Shazia Hafiz Ramji."

"before you were born" was written in a workshop with Diana Khoi Nguyen, traced from a small black-and-white photograph of my puopuo, gonggong, and mother circa 1960s. Thank you to D.M. Bradford for choosing this poem for the In(ter)ventions in the Archives contest at *The Capilano Review*.

"Rollercoasters" by Tank and the Bangas is from their album *Think Tank* (2013).

"I want to face consequences" references an anecdote in the essay "Stop Letting Trans Girls Kill Ourselves" from Kai Cheng Thom's *I Hope We Choose Love* (Arsenal Pulp Press, 2019), p. 45.

"bellytide" is a letter written to Jia Jia "Scarlett" Chen, who was killed by her mother Xuan Peng on July 12th, 2004. Italicized words are taken from Peng's guilty verdict in her manslaughter trial.

Anthony Sutton's "List of Lies" is from *Particles of a Stranger Light* (Veliz Books, 2023), pp. 34-35.

Ocean Vuong's "Someday I'll Love Ocean Vuong" is from *Night Sky with Exit Wounds* (Copper Canyon Press, 2016), p. 80.

Jia Zhangke's 2015 film *Mountains May Depart* (山河故人) comes in three chapters, each filmed in different aspect ratios representing corresponding eras: 1.33:1, 1.85:1, and 2.39:1. This poem adapts lyrics from: "酒干倘卖无" by Su Rui, Pet Shop Boys' "Go West," Teresa Teng's "甜蜜蜜," Sylvia Chang's "The Price of Love"/"爱的代价," and 康定情歌/"Kangding Love Song." The romanized Pujiang dialect of 甜蜜蜜 is created by the author, based on a YouTube cover of the song.. "The romanized Ningbo dialect phrases "tsing oh ka-go" and "weh-ling pi-fông ziang oh" come from "One Man: An excerpt from *A Primer of the Ningbo Dialect*," edited by W.A. P Martin, Henry Van Vleck Rankin, and John Luther Rankin in 1851-1857, and later curated, transcribed, and translated by Minjie Chen, Fengming Lu and Lidong Xiang in 2022.

"to alter" is from Cynthia Dewi Oka's *nomad of salt and hard water* (Dinah Press, 2012), p. 55.

Collaged words and letters from "The Industry of Caring" come from: the author's personal MCFD files from 2008, *The World of English* (January 1989), the Chinese Exclusion Act of 1923 and the Royal Commission on Chinese Immigration, 1885 via the Canadian Museum of Immigration at Pier 21, a 25 cent bill from the Dominion of Canada circa 1923, *Report on the Explosives Industry in the Dominion of Canada* (1911), *Each for Himself: Or, The Two Adventurers by Friedrich Gerstäcker* (1859), *The Shi King, the Old "Poetry Classic" of the Chinese: A Close Metrical Translation, with Annotations by William Jennings* (1891), Reminiscences of a Canadian Pioneer for the Last Fifty Years by Samuel Thompson, a draft copy of The Basic Law of the Hong Kong Special Administrative Region of the People's Republic of China (February, 1989), the Sino-British Joint Declaration on the Question of Hong Kong, *A New Student's English-Chinese Dictionary*, and *Practical Chinese Reader I*. These last four texts were acquired from the personal library of Colin and Katie Sihoe, gifted to the author by Keegan Landrigan. The text "when you joined" appears in the font Armalite Rifle.

The italicized words in "autist roams the strip malls of 3 road" are adapted from Dirty Vegas's "Days Go By."

"is it literature or deforestation" is a line that came from an earlier draft, thanks to the encouragement of Valeen Jules.

The epigraph for "Fiddling with My Chew Toy Strolling Across Matthew Wong's *River at Night* (2018)" is from Nate Freeman's "Art World Wet Paint: Jordan Wolfson Really Hates the New Jordan Wolfson Documentary, a New York Gallery Defies Quarantine, & More Juicy Art-World Gossip," in the "No-Feelings Flipper" section of *Artnet News*, May 7, 2020. The phrase "deep end" comes from a message to Matthew Wong's friend, appearing in "An Artist of Our Social Age" by Sierra Bellows in *The American Scholar.*

"Fly Like a Bird" is from Mariah Carey's *The Emancipation of Mimi*, 2005.

"Oriental Hawaii" is a tourist moniker given to Zhujiajian Island of the Zhoushan archipelagos as well as Yalong Bay in Sanya, Hainan.

"I wish I could write poems" is after Desirée Dawson's *Wild Heart* (Live from Blue Light Sessions), 2022.

"notes app apology" is after Danez Smith's "Rose" in *Homie* (Graywolf Press, 2020), p.13. "The Grandmothers" is a reference to the title given to survivors depicted in the film *The Apology* (2016) directed by Tiffany Hsiung.

Kaitlyn Boulding's "Questions to Ask Yourself Before Giving Up" is from Issue 5: Food/Land (2015) of GUTS *Canadian Feminist Magazine.*

"i want to know what comes after" quotes a Hiromi Goto tweet from November 16, 2019.

Jane Shi lives on the occupied, stolen, and unceded territories of the xʷməθkʷəy̓əm (Musqueam), Sḵwx̱wú7mesh (Squamish), and səlilwətaɬ (Tsleil-Waututh) nations. Her writing has appeared in the *Disability Visibility Project* blog, *Briarpatch Magazine*, *The Offing*, and *Queer Little Nightmares: An Anthology of Monstrous Fiction and Poetry* (Arsenal Pulp Press), among others. Jane is an alumnus of Tin House Summer Workshop, The Writer's Studio Online at Simon Fraser University, and StoryStudio Chicago. She is the winner of *The Capilano Review*'s 2022 In(ter)ventions in the Archive Contest and the author of the chapbook *Leaving Chang'e on Read* (Rahila's Ghost Press, 2022). She wants to live in a world where love is not a limited resource, land is not mined, hearts are not filched, and bodies are not violated.